Holy Matrimony

(How to Have a Successful Marriage)

DON ADAMS

Fulton Books, Inc.
Meadville, PA

Published by Fulton Books 2021

ISBN 978-1-63860-973-5 (paperback)
ISBN 978-1-63860-974-2 (digital)

Printed in the United States of America

This book is dedicated to my beautiful wife, whom I love dearly.

Her commitment to what is right and what is best for us is a never-ending process. Thank you, wife!

CONTENTS

ACKNOWLEDGMENTS

I would like to thank God and my parents for their wisdom.

Their marriage lasted fifty years.

INTRODUCTION

I have been married twice. My first wife of twenty-one years died of kidney failure.

After her death, I was determined to be a better husband if God granted me the privilege of becoming a husband again.

I remarried on December 31, 2012.

Marriage in America does not have a good success rate. Half of the American marriages end in divorce, as reported by several media outlets. Therefore, I wrote this book because I was disappointed in how I had conducted myself as a husband. Realizing that spiritual forces are at work all the time in marriages, I needed to know how to navigate with these two spiritual forces as I live with my spouse. I believe these two spiritual forces to be God and Satan. Their primary roles are to put thoughts into our minds for us to consider choosing and depending on which spiritual force we choose. We reap the benefits of what the two forces have to offer us as it relates to life. So I would like to expose conditions that the reader may or may not be aware of. Some conditions I struggled with were selfishness, bad attitude, and using God only when it was convenient. These conditions can create a rocky marriage.

I hope my experience will help you avoid pitfalls that I fell victim to in marriage and elevate you in areas that are wholesome, pure, and worthy of God's affection.

Charles G. Morris stated in his book *Psychology: An Introduction*, "Learning is the process by which experience is gained by practice or repetition." When reading this book, *Holy Matrimony (How to Have a Successful Marriage)*, some statements are repeated for learning purposes. Please understand that having a successful marriage does not mean the marriage will be free of problems or conflicts. However, having an understanding of what a marriage is up against will give you a fighting chance at winning a sustainable courtship.

CHAPTER 1

Meaning of Marriage

M

What is the meaning of marriage? Webster defines *marriage* as a legal union between husband and wife. In my opinion, marriage is a complex design from God for two people to become like-minded and devote themselves to each other's dreams and aspirations. Inside this complex arena, they must become motivated to assist each other to obtain the dreams of their hearts, preferably with God's guidance in mind.

For example, if the wife is studying to become a registered nurse and the husband has a full-time job, then the husband should make sure she does not run out of ink, paper, etc. Cook dinner, change the baby diapers if need be, and help in any way to reduce the work that is unrelated to her studies as she prepares to save lives.

In return, the wife should offer some form of relief to the husband as he assists her. It is as simple as a thank-you, "Are you okay?" or "Do you need anything?" Be careful here because what you might need from her will probably need to be scheduled. It is amazing how much further a person is willing to extend their help if they are acknowledged and appreciated. This type of tandem brings about unity and strength in the marriage.

A workload like this can also bring on stress. Although the essence of marriage is to help each other, it sometimes causes friction because one spouse is helping a lot more than the other. There is hope. It will balance out. The goal is to be aware to not attack each other. When my wife was studying to become a teacher, she had me doing everything: grocery shopping, laundry, dishes, go to Walmart for this, and go take care of that. I had my own life. I got angry at first and told her how tired I was and I was not going to do it. Then I remembered my promise to God that if he gave me the opportunity be a husband again, I would be better. Ten years ago, the old me would have said, "No, I'm tired," and I would have been stubborn with my answer. This is where I would have sided with the spiritual force that would have encouraged my actions to be selfish. I do not have the type of wife who just accepts me saying no to her. I got cursed out for telling her no and ridiculed in a royal fashion. Now I had a conflict on my mind. *Do I retaliate as suggested by an evil force (get her!) because the evil force had already suggested to her, "The nerve of him to say no, and you are doing this for the advancement of not only you but also him as well. Get him!*

Curse him out!? The conflict was "Do I respond like Jesus would expect of me or respond to the evil force suggested in my mind: *Are you going to let her talk to you like that?*" This is how arguments in the marriage starts. As a disclaimer, allow me to add that my marriage is dysfunctional. I'm okay with that because in the Bible, God told the first family, Adam and Eve, not to eat from the tree of knowledge, which reveals good and evil. When Adam and Eve ate from the tree of knowledge of good and evil, all of mankind became, in my estimation, dysfunctional. So you can be successful in a dysfunctional world.

Let's do a sidebar for a moment for clarification. America watches the NFL every year, and the Super Bowl champions are considered successful in our eyes. However, that same successful team endured challenges and pockets of dysfunctions. That team persevered through the challenges. That's where God comes in to help us through the challenges and become successful in marriage. Most married couples do not recognize that thoughts are not their own but thoughts of spirits in high places. All we can do is act on good thoughts or bad thoughts. This is the challenge or conflict of life. Now I realize that this bad spiritual force was playing me against my wife, using the most sacred and private place of my being, the mind. I chose not to advance the thought of the devil and went in to kiss her and tell her I was tired and not thinking straight. She was pulling away from me. Now I had to be careful because I was trying to do the right thing and Satan tried to get me to forget about it. But I managed to get the kiss in before I ran her errand. I realized following thoughts of the devil never lead you to a good place. Some couples end up destroying their furniture during an argument or, worse, hitting each other. "911, what is your emergency?" This is the type of ending one can expect to gain from acting on thoughts of evil.

Sir, no matter how intense the workload gets in your marriage, you must set the tone for peace and happiness, not her. Arguing shouldn't last two minutes in your home no matter what the subject matter is. Arguing is a marriage killer. I used to argue with my wife for twenty minutes or more. It would get loud and intense. It was exhausting, to say the least. There is a difference between arguing and having a discussion. With a discussion, you are more likely to reach an agreement. You are a team (one unit), not opponents. Having a successful marriage does not mean the marriage will not have conflict. Having a successful marriage means you will work with each other to be fair. In Genesis 2:23–24, Adam talks about this one unit. He says his wife is a part of him. The writer suggests that they are so connected that they should be removed from the mother and the father. This is the type of mindset you must have for marriage. This goes without saying. Be sure your spouse is the one before tying the knot. A percentage of marriages fail because one or both spouses do not detach from their parents. How do you leave the parents that raised you and took care of you for eighteen years?

Here is my opinion about why God said to leave your mother and father and cleave to your wife. God puts dreams in your parents' hearts that are designed for your parents. God has dreams for you and your wife. If your parents are the lead in designing your future, then what do you need God for? Some marriages struggle because of loyalty to their parents and even friends. I remember when I was a bachelor, I saw this beautiful full-figured woman. I told my friend I was going to talk to her. He told me not to because of her weight. I ignored him, and months later, he tried to steal her from me. In marriage, follow your heart, not loyalty to family and friends. My grandmother was impressed with a lady friend of mine when I was in my mid-twenties. The woman would bring my grandmother pies, cookies, and a financial blessing often. One day, my grandmother summoned me to her home and sat me down and told me I needed to marry that woman. My grandmother had a huge influence on me, and I couldn't ever recall saying no to her request or admonishments. That day was a turning point for me to say no to my grandmother. I knew I had to have a reason that was beyond repudiation. I told my grandmother that it would not be right for me to marry the woman because I did not love her. I don't know if she was speechless because I said no to her or that my answer was honorable. It was hard for me to go against my grandmother's wishes, but I had to do what was in the best interest of me and not her. I went on with my life. The woman remained friends with my grandmother, and my grandmother never stopped loving me. As for my marriage now, the only time my parents get involved is when my wife calls my mother and snitches on me.

She tells my wife, "PUT HIM ON THE PHONE."

That only happened once in our marriage. She uses that tool on me in our marriage ("I'm going to call your mother") to get me to toe the line. I find myself backing down when she wields that threat.

Marriage means that you develop a loyalty (bond) to your spouse stronger than your parents and friends. Let me be clear. Leaving your mother and father does not mean you discontinue a relationship with them. It means they do not have ANY power as it relates to your spouse. Their role is to offer wholesome information that may be beneficial to you. You can take it or leave it. My wife has it good. My parents take her side. She can do no wrong, it appears. I told my mother she should be more like my wife's big sister. My wife's big sister takes her side right or wrong.

My mother, being a mother, said to me, her firstborn, "I'm on the side of right!"

That's a nugget I bring to my marriage. Just strive to do what is right!

Now, if a parent or friend(s) or children have managed to disrupt the marriage, then the two of you must come together and discuss, not argue, the matter when you are calm and agreeable. Again, shouting and using profane language is not going to get you to a successful marriage. I have realized, if my wife and I are loud and angry, then the matter needs to be tabled until our heads are cool. The desire to have a resolution must be intense, not your emotion. Your desire to come to a resolution comes from love. Your emotions of anger could breed resentment. So stay calm. Most homes nowadays have a space for an office or a quiet place. It's an area that the two of you can go and discuss matters lovingly and intellectually. Find out what your spouse needs to make things right. For example, are you spending too much time and money with family and friends? At this time, a compromise must be worked out because "marriage takes work." When we got married, I shared with my wife that I send a specific amount of money to my mother monthly. I asked her, "Will that be a problem?" She said no. I have heard women talk about how their husbands will fix their mothers' washing machine while their washing machine or whatever item(s) stays broken for months. Or they give money to siblings and let their household bill or bills go lacking. The problem is, they don't discuss it with the wife.

My mother told me a couple of months after I married, "Don, don't worry about me. Take care of your home, meaning put that money into your marriage."

I told her I had already spoken to her daughter-in-law about me sending her money. Not only is she okay with it but also she encourages it. So if your money-giving story isn't going as smooth, then you need to talk. Our son loves to ask us for money. I had a discussion with my wife about how it is time to cut our grown son off from inheriting money while we are alive. I brought it up several times without arguing about it. It was hard for her as a mother to not be there when a child asked of her. I explained how I had seen so many parents grow into old age and couldn't remodel their home or drive a nice car because of children asking so much from them. After those few discussions and a misstep from our son, she now drives a nice car, and she's not looking back. Our son really feels entitled now. He wants to come visit us so he can drive the car at his leisure or, better yet, take over the car. I need to tell our son that she doesn't let me drive it and I keep gas in it and clean it. He doesn't have a chance of driving that car.

Doing this process of resolving family interference, there is a force, an adversary, that will cause trouble as the two of you try to make peace. The Bible has recorded this adversary in John 10:10. The adversary comes to steal, kill, and destroy. Satan does not want you to come together and agree. The more you agree in this dysfunctional arena, the more you give him a spiritual BLACK EYE, and the marriage becomes successful. Before you begin discussing a resolution in the meeting room, PRAY together, then begin to resolve the issue. "This takes work," and the adversary will present enough opportunities for you to get it right.

There are times when you don't get it right. The most popular weapon the adversary uses is communication. You can't resolve an issue if you don't communicate. Learn to deny evil intentions toward your spouse. Satan is always trying to play you against your spouse. This is your teammate, not your opponent. God led you to be married. The adversary hates the concept of your marriage, so he forms a thought for you to consider choosing to separate you. Once communication stops, it is easy for the adversary to steal, kill, and destroy.

Once you reach an agreement, honor it! By the way, reaching an agreement will probably never be equal. Someone will always come out ahead, and someone will get the short end of the stick.

If you agree about family involvement, then this means boundary must be set, and family is not going to settle for you choosing sides gracefully. It is okay to honor your wife's wishes and still be the man of the house. I have had guys who don't have a wife call me henpecked because of the way I honored my wife in my younger years. They wanted me to hang out with them all hours of the night. I would tell them, "She said I didn't need to be out that late. Men staying out that late are only trying to get women into bed," so they called me henpecked.

I recall a time when I played basketball in the neighborhood park years before I got married; and this guy would call us henpecked, or he would say, "I bet you wear the skirt at home."

He talked a lot of trash in this manner as someone would guard him on the basketball court. He couldn't make a basket to save his life, but the henpeck talk was plentiful. I don't know how I ended up at his home one day, but the second he entered the door, his woman lit into him like he was one of the children. And he responded to her like a child. I think the lesson for me when I look back on that day is, the heck with what friends think. They will have to cross this bridge too. You can't be intimidated about what people think of you as it relates to your family. Do what is right. Work to be fair. The message I was getting from him before I witnessed his woman's philosophy was the man should rule with an iron fist. You can honor your husband's wishes and still have equal or more power in the home. Some women are quick to label your husband a control freak if you decide to honor him. You honor him because you feel that it is the fair thing to do, given the nature of the circumstance. There is a story in the Bible about a man named Abraham. He had a wife and a maid who bore his child and lived in the same house. One day, jealousy kicked into high gear, and the wife (the one with the power) told him to put the woman and the child that he had fathered out on the streets. Abraham had spent time with the child he had fathered. There was no room for compromise.

He could have said to Sarah, "You are the one who told me to have a baby with her."

I have to think that friends hinted around the idea that if Abraham puts them out, he is henpecked! But a spiritual force (GOD) influenced Abraham to honor his wife's wishes. This is what I believe: If Abraham could control the thoughts that entered into his mind, he would have never suggested to himself, *Do as your wife asked*. It would have been a conflict of his interest. We can only act on the influence of these two spiritual thoughts of good and evil. Those two spirits are continuously soliciting our acts. So always be on guard to choose thoughts that are fair so your marriage can be successful. Being fair won't be easy, but it will be successful. You have to know when to do the right thing even when it hurts. The biggest takeaway from Abraham's action was that he played fair by doing the right thing. This man, Abraham, is not known for being henpecked. He is known as being the father of many nations because he played fair. If I had to summarize how to have a successful marriage in a dysfunctional arena, then it would be to "play fair."

There are many layers in marriage. One major layer is the concept that the man is the boss.

Since I was a child, I have heard men say, "The man is the boss! It's in the Bible" (Genesis 3:16).

Most men interpret this Bible scripture as he is the boss and he should not be contested.

Allow me to give my interpretation. As a result of Eve being tricked by the adversary, Adam and Eve got in trouble with God. They began blaming each other and the adversary, similar to what siblings do when the parent asks, "Who did this?"

So God decided, if any more problems occur in their union, then "Adam, I'm holding you responsible for the welfare of the marriage."

However, this does not mean the wife can sin against God and the husband and she won't be held accountable for it. It means that the man must say no to things that do not represent God's will. He must be the first line of defense to protect them from death and destruction and anything that hinders them from success as it relates to his family. This is where my wife backs off when she knows I'm moving in the direction of God's will, especially when I say, "It is not God's will for us to talk to each other like this. Let's shut it down" or "This particular debt will not benefit us in the grand scheme of things." You can't rule over (or boss) your family as you see fit. Husbands have an awesome mandate to guide their family into the will of God. That's responsibility and accountability. If the husband has an "I'm the boss" mentality, then there is no accountability, and God is saying in Genesis 3:16 that the husband will give an account from now on.

If shouting, hitting, and using foul language are in the home, sir, God is holding you accountable to shut Satan down, whether the adversary is influencing you or your wife. And sometimes, he influences couples simultaneously. Either way, husband, shut it down in a way that is consistent in the will of God.

Any trickery that the adversary uses in the future against your family will fall on your shoulder to annihilate him. This power to rule is for protection, not for enslaving your wife.

Typically, if the husband sees himself as the "boss" and not the protector, he will not apologize when he gets one wrong. He thinks he will look weak and it would jeopardize his position. It is God who has positioned you. As long as you are doing God's will, your position will not be jeopardized. It is when we do the wrong thing with consistency that causes us to fall into despair. We must apologize to our family when necessary. Even the wife should apologize without delay. I know it is just as hard for my wife to apologize to me when she gets one wrong. She does not like to miss the mark because it takes away her credibility to always critique me. We were at the grocery store together at the self-checkout, and she began talking to me like I was a third grader because of the way I bagged the groceries and threw them in the cart. I told her that she needed to apologize for her tone. It got worse. My insides felt like it was on fire. Rather than just respond or react angrily because of her tone, I found myself struggling to do the right thing. I chose this: I would not try to force or demand an apology from her right on the spot. This is my wife. I focused on bagging the groceries so that they would not spill back into the cart. When we got into the car, she decided to continue our episode. This is where I realized I had to take control as head of our marriage. I realized that I needed to respond to her calmly although she was in an elevated state. I acknowledged that she was right about how I handled the bagging of the groceries. I shared with her that we loved each other, and the episode was over. She responded that it wasn't over for her. I calmly asked her if she thought that this was her inheritance from past generations to be that angry over a minor detail. She realized that this question was not retaliatory because we have had discussions often about how I, as a child, took on bad habits from my father, not realizing that certain habits gained from family members are dysfunctional. It was suggested that I go to the grocery store alone from now on. We went back to the same grocery store the next week, but this time, I let her bag and tie the grocery. It went smoothly. I am proud that we did not let the devil win by separating us or trying to suggest we don't have what it takes to work together in harmony and defeat him. Men should not look at apologizing as a weakness. What if you have a daughter and she marries a man that does something that warrants an apology? Would you tell your precious daughter she doesn't need an apology because it would make her husband look weak? These are the types of games that Satan plays in our lives to hinder us from success.

Apologizing is not an act of weakness. It is an act of wisdom, courage, and love. These are the same three principles that I practiced as a university police officer over thirty years ago. I encountered some mean characters who were not students from time to time. My job description was imprinted on the badge, "peace officer" sworn in to serve and to protect. I extinguished nearly 80 percent of situations without incidents nor physical backup because I approached the situation with wisdom, courage, and love. Let me add that I was in the hood on Martin Luther King Street. I saw myself as a peace officer with the ability to annihilate entities that threatened the peace.

In marriage, you are a peacemaker. The gangster in you is reserved for taking action against the adversary with aggression and an all-out assault.

There is NO good in Satan (the adversary). Let's look at his side of the ledger:

- Kicked out of heaven with an all-out assault (Luke 10:18
- Driven into outer darkness
- Eternal fire and brimstone is his inheritance
- Despair

In God, there is good. Let's look at his side of the ledger:

- Heaven
- No crimes
- No sickness
- His glory lights up heaven.
- You will see God, his son, and the Host.
- We will live in his NEW HEAVEN for eternity via accepting the resurrected CHRIST JESUS (Romans 10:9).
- We will have mansions in this NEW HEAVEN (no mortgages). JESUS paid for your mansion on the cross.
- No electric bill
- No maintenance cost
- Love and so much more

In the initial period of getting to know my wife, I did not get the full spectrum of who she is, and vice versa. I discovered pet peeves or dislikes about my spouse. All I could do was discuss in love and NOT argue in a state of malice; "This takes work," to differentiate the two. I discussed what I disliked about her—for instance, talking to me as though I was one of her students. Also, I didn't think her out-fits were sexy enough. She claimed I gave orders or stressed demands like a drill sergeant. As nice as I am, I couldn't believe it, and her list was long and nasty. This was a particular bad habit I picked up while in the military, looking at adult sex tapes. This was one of the pastimes we did in the military. She said to throw the tapes out. She was not going to be in competition. I didn't get the "competition" part. I had to throw four or five tapes out. She said I had to get haircuts regularly and, from time to time, cook my own dinner. If she was tired, I needed to fend for myself. She told me I stink and that I needed to take three baths a day instead of two. I had to start attending church instead of only watching it on tele-vision. These are just the short list. Afterward, we laughed! And why not? No one is perfect. We needed to have this pet-peeve talk in marriage during a con-trolled environment. If you don't do it in a controlled environment, then at some point, it will come out of nowhere in a hurricane like fashion. God does not MAKE us change because he asks us to. We change because we love him, and our lives are better for it. So I gave in to her list because my life would be better for it. She left me for eight days once, and it was a good thing. I knew how to cook.

If you challenge your wife or correct your wife, you must use uplifting words. The wife cannot bear corrections. I have to be careful when it is my turn to correct my wife and not let it become a competition. It is easy to approach it as getting back at her because she thinks she is perfect. Now this is an opportunity to bring her down to the level of an equal playing field. It is never about competition in our marriage but bringing out the best actions that will promote a wholesome environment for the two of us. Wives generally believe that they are the moral authority in the marriage. It is their job to correct and not be corrected. Wives have a mental roller deck of every infraction you have done in the marriage. They will not hesitate to read to you every count like a judge sitting on the bench. The court is always in session with them. I remember a guy had mistreated our daughter. I told my wife I needed his number so he could meet me and we could have some words! She quickly reminded me how I had treated her in our college years in the late eighties and wanted to know who met with me to have some words. She explained our daughter would learn from this and she would be all right. She went from zero to one hundred to find an infraction in her mental roller deck that happened thirty years ago. So you must watch your steps as a husband. You are being scrutinized without your awareness. Have you ever noticed that when the two of you are out and about and a seemingly attractive woman crosses your vision, your wife steps back a little adjacent to your shoulder? This maneuver is to see your reaction by evaluating the eye concentration that you have fixated on the woman. Your wife will snap you out of that trance by asking, "Is that what you like?"

Here is the solution: Engage in conversation with your wife before she reads to you your rights and take your eyes off the attractive woman quickly before she asks, "Is that what you like?" By the way, she saw the woman two minutes before you did. Now, when you dare to reveal your wife's flaws, it might hurt you more than her. The nerve of her telling me to take three baths a day. Man, that hurt. In this situation, she can make you feel like a gum stuck on the bottom of a shoe. Your manhood has left the building. In your mind, you begin strategizing ways to locate your manhood. So rather than apologizing and asking for forgiveness for hurting her, you bow down to the instructions of the adversary (Satan) and make a bigger mess of the situation. At sixty-one years of age, I am trying to accept my wife's assessment of me in a way that I can thank her for showing me that. Then I let her know I'm going to work on that. I'm learning how to operate as a team and not opponents when differences attack the marriage. This counter-move "takes practice and work."

I saw an interview with the professional boxing heavyweight champion George Foreman. In the interview, you could grasp the humility he had for his wife and children. His spirit is modest and submissive to his family, yet he stands firm as head in the eyes of God; and I'm sure his family sees him strong even though he is cloaked in meekness toward his family. How does he turn off that brute ability and say, "My wife is the boss in this house"? This is showing honor and respect and leadership. He is ruling over his family as Genesis has suggested. It was revealed to me as a cadet when I was in the police academy of 1988 that police officers had a high divorce rate. These officers didn't know how to turn the brute off and turn the humility on when they got home. In John 13, Jesus washed the disciple's feet. They could not understand that a Lord, a miracle worker and a profound Spirit-filled teacher sent from God, could perform acts of a servant. Unlike George Foreman, Peter didn't know how to turn off his gangster ability and turn on meekness when required. Peter cut a man's ear off with a sword once. Peter could not deal with Jesus's meekness and submissive behavior.

Peter told Jesus, "You will never wash my feet!"

Husbands will miss the mark if they don't see themselves as a servant to their family and not the boss or a "brute." When Jesus went to the cross, he went as a servant (sacrificial Lamb) with meekness and a submissive posture for his family, which is you and me, the human race. Jesus has brutality in him. He displayed his brutality when he took the keys from Satan during his descent. Now we confess that he is Lord of lords and King of kings. This is the type of results to expect when you look at the endgame of a situation. I mentioned earlier that one person might help out more than the other person in marriage. Look how much more Jesus did for his bride (the world). It balanced out favorably for Jesus. He has a name that is above every name. Jesus has all power in his hand. He applied humility on earth and brutality against hell. I strive to be a husband in God's way, and conflict shows up from time to time. But our marriage is still logging in the years. Eight years says I'm winning like a king. My wife's laughter is in the home throughout the day and every day. This says I'm winning. Even though Adam and Eve threw us in a dysfunctional arena, we laugh a lot later about our issues. When she is talking to family or friends, laughter is always coming from her. Laughter and a healthy acceptance of one another are a value that is released when you do it in God's way. I think my wife and I have tapped into that gravity that small children find themselves in when they have differences. One minute, they are angry with each other. And in the same minute, they are the best of friends again without malice. Only our minute might take five minutes to return to being best of friends again. If laughter isn't filling the home, then I suspect the man is providing the boss- or brute-like service to his family. Laughter is associated with success. Being successful gives you power and confidence to defeat the adversary every time he tries to pull you down with him. He doesn't have an eternal mansion. He has a dark bottomless pit, and it is probably devoid of laughter.

When the pet-peeve list was over, rather than make a verbal fight of it, I looked at the pet peeves and determined her points were valid. It concerned me that she was putting up with some of the bad habits and didn't say a word until I told her she needed to dress sexier. Whenever she appeared to be hesitant about speaking her mind, I told her that this is a loving marriage. This marriage has a harm-free zone for speaking exactly what is on her mind. I feel that this is what it means when God says to rule over and not rule over her where she can't say how she feels. Just don't say how you feel in the grocery store while I'm bagging the grocery like a third grader. One day, while kidding of course, standing in the kitchen, I told her that the way it should be is, I come home from work, my dinner is on the table, and she waits for me in the bedroom. I got pinched immediately, faster than Bruce Lee could strike, the kind of pinch where women twist the skin while pinching (OUCH!). Then she bit me. I yelled "harm-free zone" for speaking my mind. We laughed while she claimed I had lost my mind. The meaning of marriage is we are a priority to each other in this world. We should operate in that priority in every present moment with love and the wisdom of God.

CHAPTER 2

Assets

A

Now that you are married, what's next? Usually, what comes immediately after is asset building. When I started writing this book about marriage, I had the young couple in mind. You have all these great ideas about becoming financially set. Unless you were left an inheritance, this idea for big money usually will take some time. For the most part, the young married couple starts with little asset and potential to gain assets. I started with one car as a husband. It was two people with two jobs and one car. So after getting an apartment, I figured, "Let's get a second car." I got tired of taking her to and from work. We needed a second car. My advice to the young couple is to stay away from the cash car. Get a certified car or a new car. My wife's first car was a new car. I never had to worry about it breaking down on her. I had bought lots of cash cars as a young bachelor. I wasted a lot of time, money, and energy doing so. A certified or new car will be fewer headaches. Many old cars require maintenance on a weekly and sometimes daily basis. A certified car or new car is one headache a month, the payment. You are building credit. Also, you need credit in America. When starting, you shouldn't max out your credit effort because the salesman tells you your credit will let you buy this beast of a vehicle. Stay on a lower affordable budget. Her new car was called the Geo Metro. They didn't come less affordable than Geo Metro. If the salesman said I had a certain amount of credit, I maxed it out. I maxed until I got into financial hardship. I had to file for bankruptcy. Man, that was a grueling process to finish. Then I was on a seven-year credit punishment as the result of filing bankruptcy.

The second asset should be a home. You will be better suited to afford a home if you are not maxed out credit-wise or if the baby decides to arrive. Buying a home is when the soliciting of credit starts to roll in. Financial problems can strain a marriage. You can find yourselves stressing out because money issues are discussed every day. That's what happened to us. As a husband, I decided to discuss financial matters one day out of the week. Then it went to once a month. I decided all the mail would be placed in one room. I found it very stressing after years of looking at bills in the kitchen, bills in the bathroom, and bills in the bedroom. Bills, bills, bills. I was young then, and I would get the mail and open it. And wherever I stopped in the house, I would put it down. If I had to do it all over again, I would have two or, at the most, three credit cards. Any number higher than that frustrates you to look at all those bills come into your home every month. Unless you have money like Wall Street, then why talk about money problems every day? I would set a start time and a time to finish. Again, it wouldn't hurt to pray first. The money meeting can become heated. Satan will try to ambush and sabotage the meeting. This is where God said the man shall rule over. You are in charge of keeping the thoughts of Satan at bay. Not telling your wife this is how it's going to be, and that's it! I summoned a meeting about my credit card being maxed out for a home project, and I wanted her to help with my maxed-out card. I told my wife, "Remember how we used to contribute $200 each every month to a project until it was completed?" She remembered, and she lit into me like an alligator dragging a deer into deep waters. That period of compromise was okay back then, but things are different now. My ego was threatened because of the way she lit into me. But the thoughts of God entered my mind. I told her this was my issue, and I heard her answer. We are teammates, not opponents. I said, "The devil will not come between us on this issue. I love you." She was mad. She can't turn her anger off that quickly. I must give her credit though. Her anger recovery time is nowhere near the length of time it used to be because as the head, I must recognize the adversary's thoughts as well as God's thoughts and choose the right course when dealing with my wife. About five minutes later,

I went to the room she was in, stuck my arm in, and waved a white napkin indicating a truce. You would have never known she was fire poker hot just five minutes earlier about me asking her to pitch in some more. So learn to commit to the start time and commit to the finish time in a meeting. Back then, we would meet again the next week to continue if we ran out of time. Do not expect all problems will be solved in one meeting. As years go by, the meeting won't be as long because you are learning your mate. You pretty much know what you can walk away with and don't even think about it. In the beginning of a marriage, I would keep notes on what we agreed on. This keeps accountability active. My wife is big on keeping notes and signing contracts. You are probably thinking that this is too much work. "Marriage takes work." You have to man up when you take the marriage plunge. After the meeting, leave money matters in the meeting and move on to living out other parts of the marriage. You have to come back together as friends like the little children do. I took charge of ending the money conversation and changing the mood. In marriage, you will have meetings, or unscheduled chaos will ensue.

With meetings, you have more control, and it could create teamwork. Once an agreement is met, it must be honored. If not, then back to chaos. Mistrust will rule the day in your marriage if agreements aren't met. My wife would remind me often when I didn't honor the agreement. Now listen closely, husbands. This should not come as a surprise. You will be helping yourself if the wife's financial needs are met first. Once her financial needs are met now, you can make the case for what you want. Although credit is a way of life for most people, you want to strive for minimizing or eliminating interest payments. The goal is minimizing debt and increasing assets.

I have heard some people say, "All you need is love."

Nope! Marriage needs money for the love and the visions to flourish.

Then there is a marriage where one or both parties are in the millionaire status. I can't speak on the millionaire level because I am not one. Although, who wouldn't want to be a millionaire? However, it is known that they have money fallouts in marriages as well. So I think the same rules apply to them as well. Sit down and talk about it. Reach an agreement and honor the agreement.

When I sat down with my wife and discussed the bills and how they would be implemented, the first question I asked was "How much money do you need a month for your maintenance cost?" I have been in the game of marriage long enough to know that wives are going to get their money. So rather than ration out $20 here, $40 there, $100 for this, and $30 for that, I asked her to total up the cost. After we set aside the tithes, the next money disbursement was for her maintenance cost. Now that a few years have passed, she asks me what I need because her career has afforded her to do so. It's a little different for me, but I'm handling this elevated generosity with happiness because God would want me to. My wife started making more money than me. Then all of a sudden, I noticed an authoritarian behavior. She started talking to me like I was a bum. She started talking to me as though I did not contribute to the cause financially. I waited a while to challenge her behavior to see if she would self-correct. As a Christian, I asked, "Did she believe she got promoted financially on her own, or did she think God had something to do with it?" Luckily, she believed in fair play also. She shut that attitude down. Whenever you are all dealing with a strong-willed woman, and this is usually every case, it must be about fairness. This is the kryptonite against them. Anything less than a "fairness" approach, your manhood will get a superman punch intellectually. By the way, I will rise again as top breadwinner. And I have learned a lesson. Don't treat people like shredded tissue because of the strength of your income.

It is good to have someone in charge of the finances. My wife is better at finances and computers than I am. I have no problem sharing with her when I need her. "You know you are better at computers than I am." I know what she is good at, and she knows what I am good at doing. The woman has not cooked a pancake in the eight years we have been married. Don't misunderstand me. She cooks and prepares many family meals. She will not cook a pancake.

She told me, "You cook pancakes better than me."

So that's why I tell her, "You know, you are better at computers than I am."

And they are both factual.

Finances are one of the leading causes of divorce. You must have a strong system for finance to have a successful marriage. It's right up there with adultery as a leading cause of divorce (steal, kill, and destroy by any means). I discuss which bill I would pay and which bill she would pay. We agreed. When one income is temporarily interrupted, it is good to have faith in God that you and your spouse will get through it. My wife and I depend on God to make a way if our finances are interrupted. We have no other plan than relying on God to see us on the other side of any financial setback.

We have seen in the news where people have decided to take their life because they had no plan for the horrific financial setback. At the time of the financial setback, I'm sure I felt pain. But the pain I felt then, I do not feel it now.

Assets are about positioning yourself to own things like as follows:

- Money accounts
- Home(s)
- Gold and precious metals
- Antiques
- Business(s) and so much more

I consider family time as an asset. I have seen several interviews with successful businessmen who regret the fragile family time. You will never gain enough money to become satisfied. Millionaires want to become billionaires, and billionaires want to become trillionaires and so on to the next status. This quest for financial gain can distract a person from matters that are more valuable than financial pursuit. Jesus the Christ said in Mark 10:25 that it is easier for a camel to go through the eye of a needle than for a rich man to enter into the kingdom of God. I had questions for God about this because what's wrong with being rich? John 10:10 says Jesus has come for man to have abundance. God himself is abundance. So, God, I need help understanding this camel business yet live in abundance. Money can't replace God. This makes God jealous. God made it possible for man to create money. Money did not create the universe. So how can we worship money more than we worship God? God will not let us in heaven if we worship money and not him. Exodus 20:3, "Thou shalt not have any gods before me." Money is powerful but not powerful enough to save your soul. So if I was mega-rich and had not received Jesus Christ for his work, then I would read Romans 10:9 and get a full understanding of this verse. I wouldn't sell all I had and give it away. I would let Romans 10:9 be my guide after this knowledge penetrated my heart. Luke 12:20 says, "Fool, this very night your soul will be required." These scriptures gave me pause in my early years of reading the Bible. Then it became clear later. "Thou shalt not have any gods before me." In the boardroom of our marriage, God is the author and finisher of our life. We represent that belief through our tithes. God has said, "Prove me," in Malachi 3:10. As I have stated earlier, money can leave you. God can give it back double. Don't let money be your god. Malachi has stood the test of time. This chase for money leaves little time for family. In my business, I have to force myself from time to time to choose family over money. There have been more times than I can count that I left home early and my wife was asleep. I came home late, and my wife was asleep on the same day. We didn't speak five words to each other on those days. It still happens on occasion, but I make sure I plan for being home early in the future. I honor it even though the business seems to spike when I tell her I will be home early. I don't know if God or the adversary stimulates the spike in my business that day, but it does not matter which one did it. I honor what I told her.

I apologized for working so late once, and she said, "Don't worry about it. Get that money."

Although she was supportive of not seeing me all day, I could see the seepage of disappointment in her eyes.

I bet someone out there is saying, "You WIMP, one day!"

I'm gone weeks at a time. Every marriage has a tolerance for being without their spouse. For some, it's a day; for some, weeks; and some, months. My marriage tolerance is a day. Unless she visits family, that tolerance is under a week. She is either returning, or I'm taking time off to reunite with my bride.

If you hear, "You are never home!" then family time is in jeopardy. Even as I write this book in my home office and the French doors are closed, if it is past 9:00 p.m. and I am still writing, my wife makes her presence known. Before she opens her mouth, I tell her, "Five minutes." You should "work" out a tolerance time that is acceptable for the two of you.

At the beginning of an ordinary marriage, money is usually scarce. Once a week or once a month, create a decent budget for date night or weekend getaways. Bills will be a constant here on earth. I wasn't going to work hard for the industries and never take out time and money for love and accomplishments. A weekend getaway can be as simple as one night at the Hilton in your city. You don't always have to leave your city or state to get away. I have spoken to several millionaires in my line of work. Many have told me how they started out ordinary, and they encourage me to believe and just keep at it.

Being young and blowing (wasting money) is normal. In marriage, money now has to be targeted. Although you work hard for the money, you do not get to spend it as you see fit. Wasting or pocket money comes after household responsibilities are met. I make it my business to be transparent about my income with my wife. This is God's way. The devil's way is to hide and hide it until the devil himself exposes one's deceit. Be honest about how much the budget will allow you to spend. Most people have this "keeping up with the Joneses" mentality. I had it, and so did my wife. This is a bad mentality for mar-

41

riage. Keep up and stay within the borders of your budget. Debt management has to be reviewed from time to time. My wife does not like to talk about her debt she has incurred. We focus now on this: Any debt created must be out of necessity and not on a whim because the credit card makes it so easy for you to fall deeper into debt. The credit card industry will raise your credit limit without you asking for an increase. This is temptation. Before you know it, you are in too deep. I focused on paying off all department store credit. This took a year of paying more than the schedule minimum payment. Next, the big boys Visa and Mastercard. Now I can persuade my wife. This freedom is liberating to the marriage.

Another asset strain is starting a business. You need your spouse on board for this. Many businessmen make this endeavor look easy and exciting. This is because they have been in the game for years. They have gone through the hard times. If your spouse is not on board, the marriage and the business could suffer. You will work harder and probably longer hours in your own business than any employer you have worked for. The important thing is to not grow too fast or borrow too much money. If a financial setback occurs, the bank will recall. I told my wife three years in advance that I would start my business. After twenty years in security, it was time to start my own thing. In the beginning of my twentieth year in security, I worked part-time in my business and full-time on the security job. I had to be realistic, especially when the banks wouldn't invest in me. Inside my twentieth year almost to the month, I went full-time in my business. And I never looked back. I've now been in business for over twenty-five years. Now I owe part, if not half, of my success to my wife. Even though she has put in minimal labor, her support in the struggle of an upstart was maximal. Without coming together, starting a business can be difficult. I witness a lot of businesses in my industry go under in less than three years because they had outrun the demand. Some complained about the lack of support from their wife and other issues. It is better to have shortage to meet the demand than to have too much borrowed inventory and no demand for it. Basically, I don't borrow more than what I need. When financial setback hits, it could wipe you out.

The financial crisis hits America about every ten years or less. This has been my experience. Family financial crisis hits sooner than ten years and sometimes more than once. So go slow and methodically.

I mentioned money and friends in the last chapter. When you begin to build assets, let's say the two of you manage to buy three cars since you have been married and a family member decides you can afford to let them take one of the cars. They are either responsible, or they are not a responsible person to be entrusted with an asset. It is as simple as that. My wife and I have a daughter and four sons. My daughter can borrow any vehicle she likes. My son, our youngest, we give him bus fare. The other sons have their own vehicles and has never asked. Do not squander your assets by allowing anyone to have access to it because you are a "good guy." Assets give you a sense of accomplishment, pride, and team-building skills. This is why God wants you to become like one body. It will create an explosion of accomplishments when you focus as a team and not opponents.

CHAPTER 3

Respect

R

Respect determines the level of joy and happiness in a marriage. Disrespect cooks up levels of sadness. Disrespect produces hurt, tears, and anger. Respect is a simple commodity. It is the act of doing what is right. I think the officiant of a wedding should ask the bride and groom, "Do you promise to respect your spouse at all costs in your union together?" Most wedding officiants will ask, "Do you promise to honor and cherish your spouse?" This statement seems to be glossed over and not piercing the heart. More times than not, the couple tying the knot is extremely happy. Then over time, the level of wedding-day joy dissipates. In the movies, we see couples who are on the verge of splitting up say a line like this, "We haven't been happy for a long time." Where did the happiness go? I believe somewhere down the line, bits and pieces of disrespect were seeded in the marriage. The human spirit's reaction to disrespect is to disrespect your spouse right back. Again, this is the adversary's way of doing business. Let's see what God says about what to do when the spouse disrespects you.

> Husbands, likewise, dwell with them with understanding, giving honor to the wife, as to the weaker vessel, and as being heirs together of the grace of life, That your prayers may not be hindered. Finally, all of you be of one mind, having compassion for one another; love as brothers, be tenderhearted, be courteous; not returning evil for evil or insult for insult, but on the contrary, blessing, knowing you were called to this, that you may inherit a blessing. (1 Peter 3:7–9)

Again, I'm convinced that we do not control the thoughts that enter our mind. This is dysfunctional. Why would I entertain disrespecting someone I married? So until we recognize these two spirits as our ongoing puppet masters in our lives, then the marriage has no chance for success. Also, the Bible puts the responsibility of being respectful in the times of disrespect on the man, not on the woman.

God has said other things too.

> For we do not wrestle against flesh and blood, but principalities, against power, against the rulers of the darkness of this age, against the spiritual hosts of wickedness in the heavenly places. Therefore take the whole armor of God, that you may be able to withstand in the evil day, and having done all, to stand. (Ephesians 6:12–13)

This inspired word of God has convinced me that we can't muster up thoughts of our own. All we can do is choose how we act on the thoughts that are coded into us from spiritual powers. Do not let Beelzebub influence you. Always remember to play fair. Fair play is never concealed. Have the courage to do what is right. This "takes work" in controlling the narrative of God. Work in tandem, using the inspired Word of God, and you will see life differently. And Beelzebub will become less and less of a threat to the inheritance that God has coded for you and your family and the generations that come after you.

At the beginning of a relationship, we put our best act on display to impress our mate. They can do no wrong in this initial meeting. We apologize quickly. We say, "Don't worry about it." We are as nice as we can be. Somewhere after three to six months, we lose that nice demeanor.

The gateway to disrespect in the marriage is when a spouse yells, "Do it yourself." The next level of disrespect is no sex, "Not tonight." This is a shock wave of disrespect. Sex, in the beginning, is usually awesome and plentiful. As the years pile up and/or children start to appear, sex takes a back seat. This is because of work, family care, or medical issues. As a man, this sex rejection hits us hard in the manhood.

Another disrespectful act is not knowing what your spouse did with the money.

"Where is the money?"

When there is a verbal conflict, we get loud. The silent treatment is another form of disrespect. These areas of unrest could lead to the ultimate disrespectful: the act of adultery. Just when things are uncomfortable and you need to get some air, you decide to get in your vehicle and drive off. Under two minutes after driving off, the adversary influences an old girlfriend whom you haven't heard from in years to call you. Is this coincidence, or is it spiritually manufactured? Not only has she called you but also her words are enticing to lure you into an adulterous affair. Now you have a choice to make. In the heat of anger toward your teammate, this appears to be justification. Let me help you with that choice. How would you feel if your wife took to the enticing words of another man? In a situation like this, you can't react selfishly. You must understand that you are being manipulated by dark forces. Politely discharge this curse by explaining you can't indulge in this type of behavior. You are being polite because the curse is not the woman, but because you deny the curse (adultery) of the adversary, you have assaulted him. And you will be better served if you ask her not to call anymore. One of the famous Ten Commandments is, you should not commit adultery. Here are three entrapments to adultery:

- Anger: When a spouse becomes angry, they seek revenge by having sex with someone else.
- Lustful desire: You either heard friends speak about a sexual act or seen acts on a screen that ignite you. You don't tell your wife that you want this type of sex because she will call you nasty. The answer is NO! So you seek sex from someone else.
- Easy access: Flirtation from someone or you decide to flirt.

I fell victim to the entrapment of anger. Before we got married in 2012, the romance was plentiful until a few months before the holy matrimony. My wife told me that menopause was at her doorstep. I have heard of menopause, but it really didn't concern me to be knowledgeable of the details. It went in one ear and out the other. She was experiencing the early stages of menopause before we got married, and I was trying to understand what happened to the plentiful romance that I was accustomed to. I got angry and started accusing her of having an affair. She was still putting on makeup, still dressing sexy, and still eating. Everything seemed normal to me. Menopause was not interrupting anything else. An old college girlfriend called me. We spoke on a few occasions before my wife and I decided to become official. I told her how I thought my then fiancée was cheating on me.

The old girlfriend said, as much as she would like to discredit her, "I highly doubt that she is cheating on you."

I told her the romance has slowed to a crawl. What I was used to receiving was absent.

She told me, "Poor baby. Get over here now!"

In my anger, I yielded to the betrayal. On the way home after the betrayal, I felt terrible. I was uncomfortable in the act. My conscience did a number on me for months before my marriage and after. The burden of my betrayal was heavy. The old girlfriend called again, again, and again. Each time, I told her about my desire to be respectful to God, myself, and my fiancée. I apologized deeply for bringing her into my drama and asked for her forgiveness.

Being a Christian herself, she said, "YEAH! God has been dealing with me also."

Man, was I relieved. For the record, we have not spoken to each other out of respect to do what is right. Most men get angry to a satanic degree because the woman they cheated with won't leave him alone so he can try to fix things with his mate. It is the devil you should be angry with. I could not be angry with neither the old girlfriend nor my wife for reminding me of my betrayal. I had to own the curse I chose to fall victim to. I am paying dues for something that should have never happened. I thank God for all the things that didn't happen as a result of my betrayal. There is a long list of things that could have gone wrong as a result of my betrayal. We made it to our wedding day on December 31, 2012. Now I am carrying a secret, and it's another heavy load on my mind. About three months into the marriage, I got angry again because of the effects of menopause my wife was going through.

I blurted out, "You must be cheating."

My wife said, "No, I'm not! You must be cheating. That's why you are accusing me."

I said with force, "I have not cheated since we've been married!"

My wife asked, "What about before we got married?"

The kitchen was so silent. The thoughts that rushed through my mind were *The marriage is over. She is going to pack her things up tonight. On one hand, I can finally let go of this secret. I have to pay her $10,000 for a breech in our relationship.*

She drew up a contract after we became engaged. In part, if one party causes destruction pending marriage, as well as in marriage, the guilty party must pay the harmed party $10,000. I explained that I was angry, and I thought she was cheating on me because the romance was not at the level when we got together.

"WHO IS SHE?"

I explained. I felt terrible for betraying her.

"WHO IS SHE?"

I promised her that as long as we are married, I will make it up to her for my betrayal.

"WHO IS SHE?"

I told her it was an old college girlfriend. I had spoken to my wife about her when we were dating and told her the involvement with the old college girlfriend did not have enough substance to manufacture a meaningful relationship. My wife's demeanor went calm in two seconds after I told her who the woman was. I continued to tell her how my conscience weighed heavily as a result of me betraying her. To this day, I have not committed adultery. I have a deep relationship with God and a seething hatred toward Satan. This keeps me focused on faithfulness. She was too calm after I told her who the woman was. I thought she would pay me back. That's why she was so calm. So as a result, I started accusing her for about a year until she packed up and left for eight days. It was the weekend of Good Friday and Easter Sunday. She finally succumbed to my intense begging to come back. I never could figure out why she was so calm the night I revealed my secret. I wanted to ask her why she was so calm that night afterward, but I knew my wife. She would want to know why I needed to know, and it would turn into something that I wished I had never brought up. The only thing I can think of as to why she was so calm that night is because it was not a woman that she despised or knew personally. This is what I tell myself because she was too calm! For the record, this is not a referendum for guys to cheat with a woman as long as your wife doesn't know the woman. For three to four years following this curse, my wife and I would discuss minor issues that border marriages.

And the slightest notion of contempt that I exhibited, she would asked, "Are you going to go out and cheat again?"

Man, the reminder of my failure hurts, and it stirred up anger. I asked God to help me. Every time she brought it up, I apologized for it. I hugged her and told her had she done that to me, I don't know if I would be as gracious as she. I told her what I told her the night the secret was broken: I will spend the rest of our married life making it up to her. I don't care if she asks me forty years from now. She will get those words. It's in her mental roller deck now. I wanted to say, "Why don't you get past this? I'm not an adulterer." I should be the last person to say this, but being accused like that is debilitating. God revealed to me that her lack of trust wasn't for her to fix. *Don't become angry because she brings up the betrayal.* This is what loomed in my thought process. Use healing gestures to mend the crack in the bond. For the past two years, she is softer and less inquisitive about my desire to disrespect the marriage in the way I disrespected the dating period. I don't get angry now when she mentions it. I only reassure her I will not betray God or her again. I assure her how much pain I felt in letting her down and letting down the

God who blesses us. I don't ever want to feel that condemnation again. As I write this, I am reminded of the countless times in my sixty-one years I have witnessed couples in public argue about how he is not cheating anymore. The guy is angry at her because he is "telling the truth." The guy is usually cursing with enthusiasm to convince the woman that he is faithful now. My advice is, if you have fallen victim to this curse and your mate has allowed the relationship to move forward, then let her be angry, not you, until you have proven your worth to her. I advise you to never get caught up in this curse of adultery or cheating on your mate. It is not worth it! I know God was behind this thought for me not to get angry at her because there isn't any peace nor righteousness in the thoughts of Satan. I really hope this helps someone. Family is a precious gem. Don't lose it. Polish it.

How many celebrities have been exposed of committing adultery, and as a result, they are severed from their family? If this isn't a curse, then what is it? How do you put a thought in your mind to be ejected from your family? The answer is you didn't; you were influenced (just as Eve was influenced in the garden and Adam and Eve were ejected). After which, the ousted husband goes into "collateral damage control" mode to become reunited with their spouse. The woman whom they had the affair with is left feeling like thrown-out trash. This is the cyclical plague that seems uncontrollable. Satan is sitting back, counting his coins because destruction just paid off. Annihilate him and refuse adultery. The flip side is, if you are not being destroyed in life, then you must be over-whelmed with the blessing from God.

I remembered a guy who had been released from prison ask me for a job years ago. Initially, I said no.

But as he walked away, I called him back. As the day went on, he told me his girlfriend threw him out of the house. After about an hour, I told him I would get him back into his home within three days. For two days, I listened to him tell me about all the women he was associated with. On the third day, he had tears in his eyes and was silent. Finally, I asked what was on his mind. He told me he found a guy's phone number in his girlfriend's purse. I started laughing.

I told him, "For two days, you have bragged about your exploits with women. And now that your woman is doing the same, you are mad!"

Now picture this. This guy had a "lot" of size on him. He was fuming. We were in a pickup truck going across an overpass that was in dire need of infrastructure repairs. The truck was rocking, and the overpass was feeling the tremors of his emotions. I did not expect him to ignite! All I could think of was *If this guy started swinging haymakers, how do I exit this truck in an instant?* Do not turn the motor off, unfasten the seat belt, and exit the door in one move. Let the truck roll on.

Fortunately, he stopped rocking from side to side, and his breathing began to regulate. My heart began to regulate as well!

I immediately went into explaining to him, "This is how your girlfriend feels when you cheat on her." I told him, "After work, your girlfriend will let you back into the house."

Throughout the day, I prayed silently for God to give me the words to say to his girlfriend to cause him to go back home. After work, he called her and told her his boss wanted to speak to her. I gave her the words God put on my heart to say to her.

She said, "Put him on the phone."

When this muscle-bound joker got off the phone, he ran to me with the joy of a toddler. I was amazed.

My advice is, do not let sex dictate your life. If you can work eight hours without sex or watch sports for four hours without sex, then you know how to occupy your time until sex from your mate is available. My wife and I went for two months without sex. Not because we were angry with each other but just to see how important sex was to the marriage. It turns out, I had more stamina and got more work done, and by the seventh week of abstinence, it was getting tough. Nevertheless, I remained faithful. Our bond is now through the roof. I do not recommend anyone to go months or weeks without sex in your marriage. My wife and I have logged in many hours of sex cultivation together before this two-month experiment. Our youngest offspring is thirty years old. We could afford a vacation or, should I say, deviation.

I do not believe that a wife should withhold sex from her husband. In America, we call that being "in the doghouse." This is punishment for crossing the line with the wife. You have been influenced. If you are disappointed with your husband, then withholding sex should not be a leverage tool. Doing this disappointing scandal, you still kiss him goodbye as he goes to work or still do things for him. You still say good night to each other. You do not shut down all facets of matrimony. You should be understanding as well. This doghouse tool is toxic in a marriage.

So even though you are disappointed with your spouse, do not forget to be respectful. You are still a team. As a sidenote to the husband, what do you do when your wife won't perform a sex act that you want? The answer is simple. You are out of luck, period. Some women are traditional and are not open to something different from their social regimen. For some churchgoing women, they believe this or that sexual activity should not go on in the marriage bed. I believe, as long as it isn't adultery and it is only the husband and the wife, then the inspired word of God found in Hebrews 13:4: "Marriage is honorable among all, and the bed undefiled, but fornicators and adulterers God will judge." This leads me to believe we can have this and that between the spouses. My understanding is, God is not judging the particulars between husband and wife only. He is judging the additional person(s) added to the (marriage bed) sexual act. That's just my interpretation. You have to read the Bible for yourself.

I have learned that anger is more readily available to the human spirit than pausing and being respectful. We are quick to dial up anger against our spouse without trying. It's immediate. This is why we find ourselves apologizing afterward when have had time to assess. I'm learning in my latter years how to assess before I speak or act. Assess whether I'm being influenced by God or Satan. In the seventies, we used to say a cliché, "The devil made me do it." We have turned his presence into a harmless myth. Satan is not a myth. We wear costumes depicting his image as fun and okay. Satan's endgame is not representative of fun and games. The endgame is destruction. It is challenging, yet at the same time, it is rewarding, defeating the circumstances that try to take me down.

CHAPTER 4

Renewal

R

Renewal is a great maintenance tool for marriage. This renewal usually comes after years of marriage. Some couples like to renew their vows. Another renewal is just doing something different. Another renewal is after a matrimonial scandal. The renewal of vows is usually cosmetics or glossed over as well. Most of the work involved in this renewal of vows is preparing the guest list, decorating the venue, then somewhere through it all, prepare on paper or, better yet, memorize some words that will mesmerize or bring the attendees to tears. Then you tell them where you are going on your second honeymoon. I call it cosmetics because after all the renewal efforts, nothing is gained or has changed in the holy union. You return to the same marriage routine.

The first thing is to review what has gone right about marriage. Extrapolate things that do not enhance the marriage. This could mean kicking grown children out of the nest. Our grown son left our home, kicking and screaming. He wasn't happy. It took some time, but he forgave us. I'm guessing he forgave us because he always tells us he loves us when we speak by phone or we visit him at the home my wife gave to the children. Decide what could be implemented into the marriage. We still help him out, but it is at a distance. This could mean attending church services or studying the Bible together in the comfort of your home for thirty minutes on a Thursday night, just the two of you. My wife and I study the Bible together on Tuesday nights. Only the two of us. We discuss the chapter, then try to relate what we have studied to our life and marriage. We contribute our "in home alone" Bible study as a major factor as to why our marriage has success today even though we live in a dysfunctional state of existence. When we have a Bible study at church with the masses, it only confirms what we have studied as a couple. This may appear to be a lot of work, but that's why marriage takes "work." The person who exercises a lot knows that it is a lot of work to stay fit. Although it is called workout, most enthusiasts do not view it as work but a lifestyle. We revere our clergymen because of their relationship with God. And we believe God speaks to them. Be assured that God speaks to all of us individually. The difference between God voicing to clergymen and to the average human being is, the clergy is responsible for enlightening themselves and the masses. As an individual, it is one-on-one.

When I was much younger, I used to wake up to a loud alarm clock. It had one volume: LOUD. For years, believe it or not, I woke up to this. Can you imagine how our day started as a result of this invasion? I bought a new alarm clock that had an adjustable sound decimal. We started waking up calmer and speaking calmer to each other. It took some time getting used to it because we were conditioned to a frantic volume. It helped start the day out calm. I made sure that the sounds weren't frantic anymore, whether it was noise from a device or each other. I shut it down. It wasn't easy, and it took a while. But I stayed calm and consistent until day by day, the morning noise was reduced to a melody. In my experience, my childhood friend's house was the same way. I would go by his home on the way to school, and as I waited for him, I could hear the mother and seldom the father sounding like a drill sergeant in the military. When I was in basic training in the ARMY, my drill sergeant didn't have anything on my mother waking us up and getting us out the door. On the opposite end of the noisy spectrum is excruciating silence. This is where a couple wakes up in the morning and punishes each other by not speaking. The first one walks out the door and never says a word. Remember when God said, "Adam, you shall rule over the wife"? It is God's intentions that when things are this heated, the man must reconcile the moment back to peace in a peaceful manner. Not speaking to each other is war. The war is against Satan, not your wife. It is hard, trust me, to walk away from being angry with your spouse at times. I've been there, and if you search for peace, you will find it. And you will benefit from that find. You can break the silence by saying "I love you." Don't expect a response. Don't let her do the job that God commanded you to perform as the husband that rules over the wife. The next time, speak again, not expecting a response. Let love rule, not your manhood. The solution doesn't come as quickly as you would like, but like everything else, you can't quit. You can't give up. You are operating in a dysfunctional arena called the Fall of Adam and Eve. When you practice this enough, it gets a little easier, and conflict is not as prevalent. Now she can see how love and understanding work. This humility comes off like weakness because society has taught us this lie, perpetrated by the enemy. Whenever you do the business of God, it is always strength. Who can stop God's lightning? Who can stop a swarm of locusts? Who can dismantle a hurdling asteroid? Who can cause a north wind to clean up an oil-stricken ocean? Jesus went to the cross for our shortcoming as well as our sins. It could seem from reading this passage that I'm letting the woman off the hook for doing her part in a righteous marriage. Not at all. In my sixty-one years, I have the revelation that God wants man to do God's will. Understand God's concept first. Then man will be better equipped to perform his duties as a husband. Don't focus on the wrong(s) of your wife. Focus on the expectation of the God who made you both. Jesus had to do this. Jesus said (after all that was going on), "Not my will, but, God, let your will be done." Jesus didn't focus on his opinion about the sustainability of mankind. This renewal of his mission was an eternal game changer. Don't focus on your opinion about your wife's actions. Understand how God wants you to perform concerning her actions. This renewal made a difference in our marriage. Renewal should make a difference.

When the yearly anniversary rolls around, the first question we usually ask is "What are we going to do this time?" I know sometimes, husbands have to be reminded of "It's our anniversary." Before planning a festive evening, take five minutes or less and ask each other, "How is the marriage for you on a scale from one to ten?" I say take five minutes or less because someone might have issues with the marriage. The issues should be short and tabled for a later discussion. This technique is tricky. You have an anniversary to celebrate. It is tricky because if the husband does not stay on task, then the two of you could start talking intensely about issues and spoil the mood for the anniversary. Unless you are seasoned in controlling the emotions that may occur, then I suggest you have this talk after the celebration. My wife and I had our "how is the marriage for you" questionnaire. It turns out, I'm a show-off. Whenever we have a family gathering and we happen to be short on supplies, I'm the first to volunteer to take care of the shortage. My wife does not like that. So she was getting heated about it and was unpacking everything about me being a show-off. I told her I'm writing down that we must discuss me being a show-off at a later time. We have our meal waiting to be picked up at Texas Roadhouse. The other question was "Is the marriage in a place that you are willing to stay in till death parts us?" We both agreed that it was stable enough. The last one was "What would you like to see improved?" You don't want more than three or four questions raised when using this technique because it may take a year or two to get results. My wife only had two complaints out of eight years of marriage: me being a show-off and me crying victim after I provoke her over something silly. For instance, I sneak up behind her and grab parts of her body without her signing off on it, and she turns and pops me in the head with a wooden serving spoon. Or it could be as easy as a loving smile, and everything is great.

The one problem you will have when operating a marriage like this is perceived boredom. Be careful not to dismiss wholesome marriage with boredom. The wholesome marriage life can be repetitious and seems at times "dull." However, so can unhealthy drama become repetitious. We see unhealthy drama played out through our family, television, and other means. I rather have a repetitious wholesome marriage than a repetitious drama-filled marriage. I think this is why vacations were implemented. Listen to Galatians 6:8–9: "For who sows to his flesh will of the flesh reap corruption, but he who sows to the Spirit will of the Spirit reap everlasting life. And let us not grow weary while doing good, for in due season we shall reap if we do not lose heart." Drama is usually a corruption. Wholesome marriages can get boring, but the lifestyle produces a good harvest (long-lasting marriages). The marriage between God and man/woman is dysfunctional, but Christians are not divorcing God. And God is not divorcing Christians. This marriage has gone on since Adam and Eve. We separated for a while, doing "Noah and the ark" days, but we got back together. And now we are together for eternity.

How do you renew the marriage after a scandal? The first process is the act of forgiveness. I was lucky. My fiancée at the time did not have to keep the relationship going nor forgive me for my actions. Just because I said I was sorry does not mean she had to recoil back to the way it was. Everything must be focused on renewal and repair. It's not as easy as "It happened. It's over. Let's move on." This scandal repair or renewal can take years. These days, I can't afford a misstep or a scandal because I'm working overtime in the renewal process. At first, it was frustrating because reconciliation (trust) didn't return quick enough. It made me want to quit, and it made me angry at time. I took the focus off myself and focused on whatever it takes to make the family whole again. I broke it! Even though my fiancée was going through the early stage of menopause, I made a vow in sickness and in health, and I broke it! Taking stock and taking ownership helped to heal me and create a smooth transition to begin reparations.

We remodeled the floors in our home. Well, we hired professionals to do the job. This was a renewal for us that it is a daily refreshment to see new floors instead of the old floors.

One of the hardest things to renew is the state of mind. I am jealous about my wife to the point that it gets unnecessary. Not only is it hard to renew this jealous behavior but it is also hard to write about it. I don't like my wife laughing it up too long with any man other than her family. If we are at a gathering, it gets to the point that I feel like "Did she forget I'm here too?" We are so close that it feels weird not being in close proximity after a certain time at any gathering. It is not easy to enter into our bubble and manipulate our time individually. So my wife tells me I'm too jealous. So I work on renewing my position on trust. When I realized that I was set in my ways, I tried to understand. When did I become this jealous person? And sure enough, repressed memories of relationships in the past showed clues for jealousy. When I was in the eighth grade, there was this girl I liked. She had me carry her books as we walked to school. One day, she told me to go to the store and buy her a package of Doublemint gum and hurry back before she made it to class. This was the day I found out I could run fast. I made it back to her midway on the school ground. She opened the gum, got a stick for herself, then gave a stick to a boy I had never seen before. I waited for her to give me a stick of the gum that I used part of my lunch money to buy, and she never gave me a stick of gum. I had to skip lunch that day because I was short a nickel. I haven't fixed the jealousy yet, but I'm getting better. I don't want to be a person who doesn't have some jealousy. God himself says he is a jealous God. But I want the proper measure of jealousy. So what does a proper measure of jealousy look like? For me, I should care that my spouse's affection is reserved for me. My spouse should not fear that I will have an insane outburst over her laughing too long with some guy. My wife should not fear wearing something sexy when she leaves the house and I'm not with her. Now, when I say, "Wear something sexy," I don't mean something outrageous. Truth be told, I want her representing me well. However, there is a point where if I'm laughing it up with a woman too long or she is laughing it up with a gentleman in excess, it can be disrespectful. I should not assume though because she is personable or a likable person and that I should be jealous.

Lord knows I have had some bachelor experiences where I was laughing it up with a woman, and when I made advances, she said, "Sorry, dude. I didn't mean to give you that impression."

There is nothing happening here. And for the record, my wife has jealousy issues as well. She grabbed me one time where a woman with fingernails should never grab a man. Jealousy kicked in, and I was lucky enough to produce proper information to disengage her death grip. I thought she didn't want to be married anymore because of how things had changed, and I said I would release her from marriage without conflict. I would be all right and find someone who wanted to be married to me. This was a year after I had confessed to the betrayal. She wasn't calm like before, and I hadn't betrayed her. Honestly, I thought maybe she wasn't happy anymore. Now I know marriage does not have to have whistles, balloons and confetti, and sex flowing all the time for a marriage to be happy. Just be there and be there with faithful intentions. For the record, the age that my wife and I are at does not require an overdose of fun. Like many, we overdosed on fun in our early years. The things we consider fun now are fishing, our careers, paying our bills on time, getting together with siblings and children during holidays or birthdays, enjoying our home, vacations, her Cadillac, my Dodge Ram, studying the Bible together, matching wits with each other on a daily basis, eating out, going to church, shopping, dancing together at weddings, and receiving unexpected monies. This lifestyle maybe a little boring to some, but at our age, it is fine with us.

Integrity

I

Integrity is a challenging force. When we are alone and faced with the act of integrity, we would help ourselves if we meet the challenge. We should do what is right even when no one is looking. We could lose ourselves in the act of doing what is wrong. Let me explain. They say we should not judge a book by its cover as it relates to people. But some people are unmistakably a "bad apple." Just one look at their aura, and you sense the nature of them. The question is, How did they get that "bad apple" radiation? They have failed the challenges of integrity when presented to them time and time again. It emanates from them before they open their mouth.

I try to reveal as much as I can to my wife when it comes to where I'm going, what I plan to do, and what my intentions are often. For instance, I told her early in our marriage that I was headed to the bank and I would be right back.

She told me, "You don't have to tell me that. I'm not your mother."

For me, I know who my mother is (she is such a wonderful and lovely woman). What I attempted to do in the marriage was to establish a path of integrity. I work on being proactive when it comes to transparency in the marriage. At the time, my wife felt that it was too much information. Over the years, she has grown to appreciate the information. Just because you are grown does not mean you don't give an account to your spouse. It's not that you need permission like a child. It's integrity placed as guardrails to assist in a wholesome marriage. Without integrity, your marriage could radiate like a "bad apple." Integrity is tied into all facets of marriage. If you keep secrets from your spouse, it will affect you personally and the marriage. I know society is big on you to have some secrets, but God does not want marriages guided by popular society. He wants the righteous (Christians) leading the way. When the Christians yield to the lack of integrity, then what hope does popular society have when guidance is sought? Christians should lead the way in wholesome, long-lasting marriages. When popular society sees the success among the Christians, they should look to what we are doing to be successful. That's how integrity plays a role also. It inspires and encourages. This was one of Jesus's missions: to encourage the world to see things his way and use believers to become disciples of his calling. Joseph in the Bible was a man of integrity. If Satan had integrity, he would not have been cast out of heaven. He is now unstable. Integrity creates stability in marriage. Integrity is a hardworking tool that can be useful in many things. My wife can have a question like "What did you do with the money you made this month? I don't see the fruits of it." Personally, I was offended. If I would have taken the offense route, the matter would have gotten worse. First, I spoke that it would not be good for marriage if I misappropriate funds. Then I produced the spreadsheet and receipts. Everything added up, and it was smooth sailing. As I write this, the biggest take-away was, I stayed calm and confident. I was proud of the outcome. In the eight years that we have been married, this "Where did the money go?" inquiry has only happened three times. I think it was more of an integrity evaluation of me than the money trail. She wanted to see how I would respond. Women are major sleuths in matters of gaining insights. The more they already know, the less pop-up inspections. So I don't keep secrets. Again, it is better to be proactive with integrity. If the husband's integrity is intact, then these surprise inspections won't hurt you. I do not encourage wives to start pop-up inspections of your husband. What I would encourage is reading the Bible and praying together before testing your spouse in areas that maybe questionable. You do not want to open a potential can of worms without the lifeline of a spiritual buffer. When integrity is put on trial in my marriage, the trial never lasts long because my integrity shuts down improprieties. I am not perfect. We all know no one is perfect thanks to Adam and Eve.

Another function of integrity is when you get one wrong. Integrity allows you to take ownership and vow to fix it. I pondered on the difference between integrity and the love for God. For instance, I choose not to commit adultery. Is that integrity or my love for God? I have found that learning of God produces integrity. When I struggle with something, I work in God's way of doing things, and it will break the stranglehold that sometimes grips me from living free. I once had a woman call me a "punk," attacking my manhood because I refused to continue a relationship with her. I was able to pursue my life of freedom because of my love for God. Without this buffer (love for God), it is difficult to convict to principles that will not plague or plaster me to bondage. I had a customer talk to me about him trying to be faithful to his wife, but the women at his church kept pulling him back in. I believe he wanted to be faithful. His problem was his love for God and integrity. Whether it is women, drugs, or whatever, when I developed a love for God more than the desire for an addiction, I became successful and free. I have several things I'm working on in order to improve my life, but they are not things that could destroy my marriage in a blink of an eye.

Things that can end a marriage in a blink of an eye are as follows:

1. Anger—Strong inappropriate language; physical fights. Remedy: Be strong and resist this emotion.
2. Money discrepancy—Income spent on things not associated with securing the marriage. Remedy: Spend money appropriately. Talk it out with your spouse.
3. Adultery—Sex with someone other than your spouse. Remedy: Indulge in your spouse only.
4. Constant lies—Information not consistent with the strength to bind the marriage. Remedy: Tell the truth.
5. Communication deficit—Refusing to talk with substance to bind the marriage. Remedy: Express yourself calmly. Be fair with your words.
6. Unforgiveness—Mentality complex of "king versus subject": "Who do you think you are to hurt me and walk away without retribution?" Remedy: Swallow your pride. Absorb the pain with the sponge called love. Work it out. No one is perfect.
7. Punishment tactics—Making the spouse feel worthless. Remedy: Consult with God on how to move in a direction other than inflicting pain at all costs on your spouse. God will give a solution to your brain to

execute that will reflect wholesomeness if you ask.

8. Disappearance—Gone without adjudication; unauthorized absence; AWOL. Remedy: Open up and take a time-out to tackle differences.

9. Spousal neglect—In an individual bubble; at-home or in a group setting. One spouse is totally disengaged in the marriage. Remedy: Stay engaged. A slight touch of hands; a smile. Buy their favorite dessert. This confirms spouses may not be in a good place now, but we will get pass this.

10. Incompatibility—Usually, incompatibility shows up after the "just-having-fun runs out" (the annulment), having never discussed issues on any kind. She or he was so cute; let's get married. Or their house is so nice; let's get married. And you run to the altar full of surface appearance and later find out that you do not have enough "common interest" currency to buy a ticket for a long-lasting marriage. Remedy: Take time to identify people and activities in a potential marriage partner.

We have adult children before she and I married eight years ago. She has four children. I have a son in addition to the one my wife and I have together. My primary goal was not focused on her children liking me. They would have seen through the fakeness immediately. I shared with her children at a celebration where our daughter got her first master's degree that my primary mission as their mother's husband was to make her happy and they need not worry about her. Since that day until now, I know they have respect for me because of my integrity that goes into making their mother happy. I know they have respect for me by the way they each absorb information that I share with them that may be beneficial to them. The biggest respect is when they share "I love you all." This couldn't be possible if integrity is missing. Let me add. As a person marrying into a family, you must pile on integrity thick and heavy in your "actions" as much as you can. It's been eight years, and her children are "starting" to see me as legitimate. Well, the jury is still out with "Daughter!" She still has the "I'm watching you" demeanor, but I'm not concerned at all. My love is godly. It's good to have someone hold you accountable. She is working too hard because God himself is holding me accountable. (Man shall rule over the wife. Man is accountable unto God.) It also helps that their baby brother (who is thirty years old) is my son. I'm not concerned with scoring points with the children. I want to cement a legacy of "family man" that could be passed down through generations. This integrity does not come overnight. It is always ongoing. One must have integrity in order for something to last.

CHAPTER 6

Anointing

A

The anointing is the unmatched spiritual power that is possessed by God the Trinity.

The heavens and all things created were manifested through God's anointing ability.

> I am the Lord, and there is no other; there is no God besides me. (Isaiah 45:5)

> For thus said the Lord, Who created the heavens, Who is God, Who formed the earth and made it, Who established it, Who did not create it in vain, Who formed it to be inhabited: I am the Lord, and there is no other. (Isaiah 45:18)

In the beginning God created
the Heavens and the earth.
(Genesis 1:1)

The ability to create this universe was God's anointing power. God raised Jesus from the dead with his anointing power. So why is the anointing relevant to marriage? Marriage is holy. Good things should dominate and gravitate to marriage. You and your spouse must collectively EXPECT your dreams to come to pass because of the anointing power of God. In Psalm 100:3, it says it is God who has created us and not we ourselves. In marriage, if we follow the guidelines of God, we can create and we can have the coded dreams of our hearts through faith in God's anointing power. The thing about this anointing power is, it is not a magic trick. God possesses this anointing power. We can't possess it. However, we can tap into his anointing. I feel this way because a woman in the Bible touched the cloth of Jesus, and she was cured. Jesus claimed that the anointing (virtue) left his body because of her faith that the anointing power that he had could heal her; Jesus had to meet this woman because she did not reveal herself before touching his clothes. Jesus was conditioned to people coming to him, and they responded to his questions, "Do you believe…" And when they answered, he granted their petitions. This woman didn't fill out the questionnaire. She just tapped into the power of anointing from Jesus for a moment to be healed. When she tapped into the anointing and was healed, she wasn't possessed with it. If the woman was possessed with it, we would hear about other things she did as well. So this tells me that as Jesus walked this earth, he did not possess the anointing. He just taps into it. This is why Jesus said in John 14:12, "Greater works shall we do also." God possesses the anointing. No matter how much faith we have, we can never drain the anointing out of God like the woman drained the anointing out of Jesus. If Jesus possessed the anointing on the cross, he would have never died because of the anointing. There is no death in the anointing. God is the alpha and the omega, the beginning and the end. God can never die. However, Jesus is alive forevermore now!

It was the anointing (the Holy Spirit) that bore Mary's womb and birthed Jesus. It was the anointing that opened the Red Sea and allowed the Israelites to cross over to the other side. It was the anointing that God blew into man's nostrils that made him a living soul. It was the anointing that allowed Jesus to walk on water. With this mustard-seed amount of knowledge about the power of the anointing, possessed by God, husbands, you can navigate your marriage to GREAT heights. The use of the anointing in man's life is limited to the advancement of liberating mankind to worship God for who he is to mankind and worship him without fear of an enemy and live life in abundance. Tapping into the anointing is not for what Satan tried to do or the Babylonians tried to do in (Genesis 11:4). Satan tried to overthrow God. The Babylonians tried to build a tower to heaven. Acts 1:9 says Jesus went back to heaven in a cloud. The cloud was anointed. Use the anointing to assist you in overthrowing obstacles in your marriage and everyday living. Engineers around the world build elaborate spacecraft to journey space. By all means, travel space. Explore the wonders of God. However, God does not need mankind trying to get into heaven any other way than through Jesus Christ. Jesus said, "I am the door in which to get into heaven" (John 10:9). God doesn't need any help nor does he need us trying to figure out how to show up in heaven unannounced (crashing the party). You will end up like the Babylonians, confused and going around in circles until you find your way back to worship. Tapping into God's anointing power should empower us to know we can overcome situations that plague us as humans. Marriages should blossom bountifully because we exercise this gift. When I operate in this reality, things get better. My challenge is to not become detached from the anointing because of setbacks or dilemmas. For instance, in the Bible, the Jewish people kept getting into trouble in the wilderness after the anointing power of God opened the Red Sea. Stay with the anointing power of God no matter what. God gives us a lot of things. Some things we abuse. The good thing about God's anointing is, it can't be abused. We can't abuse the anointing by creating our own universe as he did. We can't abuse the anointing by making ourselves supreme spirits subject to no equal. No one is equal to God because of his monopoly on the anointing.

We can only go so far with God's disbursement of anointment. It is healthy to know the purpose of the anointing. The anointing can create worlds. But for us, the anointing is limited. It is for liberating mankind to worship God without restraint. If my marriage were to have restraints, I believe that restraint or burden can be removed by faith in the anointing power of God. This gives me the confidence to worship him in spirit and in truth. Satan's failure to overthrow God was because he has no anointing abilities and never did. When my marriage is attacked, the anointing is my advantage. I can tap into God's anointing, or I can try to work it out on my own. To tap into God's anointing power is through reading the Bible and trial and error. Also, a personal relationship is required with God in order to tap into his anointing. Pharaoh's men had powers of sorcery, but their powers were not anointed. Other sorcerers knew the secrets of their trade. No one has a clue to God's origin concerning the anointing. NASA struggle with the big bang because they use pen and paper as well as equations to answer the question of how the big bang banged. The anointing power of God that caused the big bang can't be defined nor be revealed by human's limited knowledge, and it never will. That is not what the anointing is for. For the record, I love NASA. NASA television shows reveals information about God through their explorations that are equal to preachers in my estimation.

CHAPTER 7

God

G

Who is God? God is a spirit that no man can define accurately. It is just as difficult to define who God is as is for team NASA to define the absolute of SPACE. Once you think you know who God is, more information is released for exploration. In our vernacular, one of the best ways to describe God is that he is a mystery. In this mystery, from the best that I can tell, there are things about God that are not revealed to us because it is not relevant to us. However, what is relevant to us as creatures made by God is that he wanted a spirit, unlike the spirits he has around him, that sees him every day to worship him.

This spirit is designed to believe in him even though we can't see him. You have to develop love and trust in this experiment. As long as we follow the will of his spirit, we can inherit the confidence that he is all that he confesses himself to be in our hearts and in the inspired Word of God (the Bible). As intellectuals, whatever a man designs, he can produce a manuscript to show you how the product was made. With our intellect, we do not know where to begin to describe nor create anything equal to God's creations.

Anything that man has developed throughout life, it is God who created the substance for a man to begin formulating. The spacecraft, the technology, the shelter, the food, the liquids, the fabrics, and the list goes on. God put these materials out here for us to enhance our lives and to worship him in an abundance of luxury. The idea of God was to create a spiritual being that will worship him by choice and give them no visible information about his physical existence. As a result of this idea, we will see his promise to us come to pass. Rather than release the promise instantly, God has inserted time and progression. Without the experience of uncertainty, this idea would be futile. Jesus always said, "If you believe and not 'doubt' [uncertainty], then God will give you what you ask." So yes, God has placed stipulations on this concept to worship him. With this stipulation, we are calculated to worship him in pure honesty.

My wife and I pray to this God to guide and bless our marriage. We try to incorporate God in all that we set out to do.

We know that our church has a Wednesday night Bible study. But my wife and I study the Bible on Tuesday nights. We study one chapter at a time. In our seven-plus years of marriage, we are now in the book of Ezra. (Inserted: December 31, 2020: We are now in the book of Job.) I told her a few years back that it will be twenty years before we finish reading the Bible at this rate.

She asked me, "What's the problem? Where are you going? You have somewhere to be?"

Thank God I came to Christ in my thirties. As a result, I have read the Bible from cover to cover on my own three times. Also, I refer to the Bible throughout my life for references and when the preacher on a Sunday morning tells me to turn to the book of…

God wants to go on the journey of our lives. He knows difficult times will pursue and invade our lives.

He asks, "Is there anything too hard for me?" (Jeremiah 32:27).

In this journey with God, he will see you through invasions and get you back on track to good times and abundance. He wants to go through the journey of good times as well. Remember, God is anointed, not appointed as leaders of a nation. Appointed leaders all have an end. God is here for you and your generations. God picks which egg enters a mother's womb. God told Jeremiah he knew who he was before he called dibs on his mother's womb. By now, we are aware of the general knowledge that many eggs are in the hunt for the incubator. And the one(s) that make it, God already knows. Are you starting to get a revelation of who God is? He is able. How did God create himself? This question is rhetorical. I do not want to waste my time at sixty-one years of age going around in circles, trying to figure out how God came into existence. The question was slated to give more insight into who God is and his ability. Nothing created God. Yet God created everything known and unknown to man.

CHAPTER 8

Endless Love

E

What is endless love? Why do we need it? How do we get it?

Endless love is a continuous emotion that is activated by action(s). Endless love is pure. It is the God kind of love (agape). This love is unconditional. God's love is available to all. There is a price for rejecting God's love (Jesus Christ). Jesus was criticized for socializing with sinners. He was operating in his assignment from God, exercising unconditional love to the Jews and the Gentiles.

Conditional love has an end. You don't want conditional love in a marriage. Some people love because of money, power, etc. When the money, power, etc. run out, so does the love. Agape love stays. It is endless. This endless love performs in forgiveness, helpfulness, care, support, constructive chastising, education, and more. In John 3:16, it says, "For

God so love the world that he gave his only begotten son, that whoever believes in him should not perish but have everlasting life." This endless love is a two-way street. One person can't do all, performing love and creating an endless love.

Even babies that can't talk return the love with the smile from their eyes and mouth and from the unconditioned kick of their legs when love is shown to them.

Judas betrayed Jesus. Peter denied knowing Jesus on three recorded occasions. Jesus asked God to forgive the people who hung him on a cross and mocked him. In marriage, this is the kind of action we must be prepared to express. Hopefully, we won't have to experience the extreme because we know right from wrong.

There are times when I come home, I notice dishes are piled up or the laundry has piled up. They are usually taken care of. I clean up the area. Sometimes, we do it together. These are simple actions of love. There are times when you inconvenience yourself and do things out of love. My wife and I have a system in our home. I'm responsible for the maintenance outside, and she takes on the maintenance inside. Sometimes, I take on both because she is really exhausted and so am I. I don't fuss about it because I am the head (servant).

Jesus fasted for forty days for us. He loves us endlessly. Pray for your wife. Anoint her head with oil if you believe in that and pray for her. It does not have to be for forty days. Just pray over her from time to time. This is endless love.

When something is inappropriate in a marriage, then you need to say something. The scribes and Pharisee were more of a status in the community rather than servants to God's people. They enjoyed the love of power. When Jesus came along, he chastised them for their lack of concern. No endless love flourishes without a little correction from time to time. Be an educator and not a dictator.

We need endless love because of its nutritional value to the human spirit. Growth and progress can come out of endless love. With growth and progress, we can compile a useful and sizeable inheritance.

Family reunions are the product of endless love. If no one loves, then no one shows up at the reunion. We all know how much fun (nutritional) family reunions bring to the human spirit.

When America has a crisis and all its citizens come together to assist his or her neighbor every time, this is the endless love indoctrinated to nourish the human spirit. Without this value, we would be identical to the priest and the Levite who walked past a human being in need in the Bible. As a whole, we are a family—a good Samaritan spirit. What is a family without love? It is a disconnection. This disconnection of lacking love for one another germinates a societal rot.

The way we get this endless love is through learning the Word of God. By tapping into the will of God, he will reveal in our hearts and minds what we should act out. If we choose to not read the Bible, then love can only take us so far because we don't have access to the anointing. In our strength, our indoctrinated love isn't planted in the soil of God's will to produce a bountiful harvest. Just like a seed that isn't planted in proper soil. It's a seed, but it can only go so far because it is not connected to the thing that causes growth and expansion to its fullest capacity. To love properly, you must be connected to the endless lover.

ABOUT THE AUTHOR

Don Adams has been a lover of God for over thirty years. As the oldest of six children, Don and his siblings have experienced the ups and downs of a marriage by watching their parents. Although his marriage has not been picture-perfect because of failures and shortcomings, he owes his success to Christ Jesus. Therefore, Don credits the longevity of his marriage to one-on-one Bible studies with his wife. Don also had the privilege of teaching in prison ministry with his local church with the emphasis on marriage and family.

He is the father of two biological sons and have three bonus children. He presently resides in Dallas, Texas, with his wife of nearly ten years. Don enjoys traveling with his bride and spending time with his children, grandchildren, and great-grandchildren.

CPSIA information can be obtained
at www.ICGtesting.com
Printed in the USA
BVHW031536050122
625453BV00004B/406

9 781638 609735